What Jesus Really Taught
(And Why We Don't Believe It)

What Jesus Really Taught (And Why We Don't Believe It)

©2004 Mark W. Lansberry
All Rights Reserved
ISBN 0-9763479-0-3

Cover Photo: Todd Bolen/BiblePlaces.com
Used by permission.

"He tells what he has seen and heard,
but how few believe what he tells them!"
– John 3:32 (NLT)

Scripture References:

KJV	*King James Version*
ISVNT	*International Standard Version*
	Parsons Theology, 1999
NLT	*New Living Translation*
	Tyndale House Publishers, 1996
NRSV	*New Revised Standard Version*
	Zondervan, 1990
TMSG	*The Message*
	Navpress, 1993

Contents

Introduction	1
1. *Listen!*	3
2. *Follow Me!*	9
3. *Wake Up!*	13
4. *Look!*	17
5. *Step Out!*	27
6. *Worship!*	34
7. *Care!*	41
8. *Be Perfect!*	48
9. *Practice!*	56
10. *Share!*	63
11. *Go!*	69
12. *Live Life Abundantly!*	74

Introduction

This is a book about spirituality. It is not a book about religion. In particular, it is about the spirituality taught by Jesus. It is through our spirituality that we discover our connection with the living God. "God is spirit and those who worship him must worship him in spirit and in truth." (John 4:24 [NRSV]) Jesus taught a very real and vital spirituality, a spirituality that transforms our very lives. "The wind blows where it chooses, and you hear the sound of it, but you do not know where it comes from or where it goes. So it is with everyone who is born of the Spirit" (John 3:8 [NRSV]).

Religion on the other hand, tends to be static. It is a system of ideas about God and about spirituality without necessarily requiring or leading to a direct realization of either. Most Christians today practice a religion about Jesus with the emphasis on his sacrificial death on our behalf and very little attention given to what he actually taught during his ministry.

While the importance of Jesus' death for our sake cannot be over-emphasized, Jesus' teachings are also important. It is his teaching about spirituality that prepares us for life in the kingdom of God. And, importantly, Jesus teaches us that that life begins now, in this world. If we don't understand our own spirituality in this life, we will enter the next unprepared for the fullness of God's kingdom. This book seeks to recover what Jesus taught during his ministry that leads us to a vital spirituality – the abundant life he came to offer us.

Chapter One
Listen!

When I was growing up, like most baby boomers, I loved rock and roll. I was mesmerized by the Beatles, the Rolling Stones, the Mamas and the Papas, The Loving Spoonful, etc. I played and sang their songs night and day. And, I thought classical music was boring. I suffered through music appreciation classes wondering how anybody could stand to listen to the stuff. There was no beat, no electric guitars, and no teenage angst-filled lyrics.

My love for rock and roll led me to take up the guitar and play in a number of garage bands. I loved to play the music even though I wasn't particularly talented. When I went to college after serving in the Navy, I decided that I would major in music since that was my first love. To my dismay, I learned that the university did not offer a major in rock and roll, nor even in the guitar.

No more daunted by this than by the fact that I wasn't particularly talented, I went ahead and majored in music theory and composition. As I studied the great composers and their music, to my surprise and delight, I fell in love with the music of Beethoven, Mozart, Bach, Brahms, Schubert,

Bartok and countless others. I discovered a new world, rich with harmonic and rhythmic nuances that I had failed to appreciate. Largely because I had never really heard them before. But, now they were part of my world, part of my consciousness.

My experience with classical music is similar to the way most of us have experienced the gospel of Jesus, even though that message has been around even longer than the music of the great composers. We have never really grasped the message Jesus taught, largely because we have never really heard it. You may be inclined to disagree with me and say that you have heard the message and do believe it. Of course, I cannot speak to any individual's personal experience. But, the members of our society in general do not really believe it.

What we really believe determines how we live our lives. For example, if we believe that an airplane can fly us from New York to Paris we are willing to get on the plane. If we don't believe that, we won't. Indeed, there are persons who refuse to fly because at a deep level they don't believe they will arrive safely. Another example, if we believe that our car will start and we can drive the distance to our doctor's office in twenty minutes, we plan our schedule to allow us that amount of time to get to an appointment. What we really believe informs the way we live our lives.

So if we really believe the message of Jesus, there ought to be a discernible difference in our lives as a result. However, in December of 1983, the Princeton Religion Research Center published a survey conducted by the Gallup Organization. The researchers measured a wide range of moral and ethical behaviors such as calling in sick when not sick, cheating on income tax, and pilfering company supplies for personal use. What they found most startling was that there was no significant difference between the churched and the unchurched in their ethics and values on the job.

Jesus came to us heralded as the Prince of Peace, to bring peace on earth and good will to all persons. He taught us to "love your enemies, do good to those who hate you, bless those who curse you, pray for those who abuse you. If anyone strikes you on the cheek, offer the other also; and from anyone who takes away your coat do not withhold even your shirt. Give to everyone who begs from you; and if anyone takes away your goods, do not ask for them again. Do to others as you would have them do to you" (Luke 6:27-31 [NRSV]). If we really believe what Jesus taught, how do we reconcile this teaching with the obvious fact that there is no peace on earth?

In my life time, my country alone, the United States, has engaged in wars or military interventions in Korea, Viet Nam, El Salvador, Granada, Somalia, Iraq, Bosnia, Afghanistan, and Haiti. Prisons in our country are over crowded. In my home in Maricopa County, Arizona, our sheriff has erected tents to house inmates because there are not enough jail cells. Our civil courts are backed up for years with people suing one another. The Catholic Church in this country has been rocked by the scandal of priests sexually abusing young people in their parishes. Road rage moves complete strangers on our roadways into hostile confrontations that sometimes result in death.

Where is this peace that Jesus offers us? "Peace I leave with you; my peace I give unto you" (John 14:27 NRSV]). If we were really living the way Jesus taught us, you would think that after 2,000 years we would be more peaceful and loving and that would show in the world around us. The problem is we don't really believe it, because we haven't really heard it.

We're like the housework-challenged husband who decided to wash his sweatshirt. Seconds after he stepped into the laundry room, he shouted, "What setting do I use on the washing machine?"

"It depends," the wife replied. "What does it say on your shirt?"

He immediately yelled back, "Arizona State University."

Of course, this is nothing new. Even those closest to Jesus, his family and his disciples, had trouble understanding him: "His brothers were pushing him like this because they didn't believe in him either" (John 7:5 [TMSG]). "But they didn't get it, could make neither heads nor tails of what he was talking about" (Luke 18:34 [TMSG]). "Then

Jesus made it clear to his disciples that it was now necessary for him to go to Jerusalem, submit to an ordeal of suffering at the hands of the religious leaders, be killed, and then on the third day be raised up alive. Peter took him in hand, protesting, 'Impossible, Master! That can never be!'" (Matthew 16:21-22 [TMSG]).

We still have trouble understanding and believing what Jesus said.

I invite you to discover anew for yourself what Jesus taught. You may want to set aside for the time being everything you think you know or believe that Jesus taught, and let his words speak to you.

In the television series "Kung Fu," Kwai-Chang Cain, a Chinese-American priest, who is an expert in the martial art of Kung Fu is hiding out in this country in the 1880's because he killed the emperor's son in China. During each episode there is a flashback to Kwai-Chang's childhood, growing up in a Shaolin temple. Often these flashbacks feature the boy in dialogue with his blind mentor, Master Po, who always fondly calls the boy, "Grasshopper."

In one episode, it is explained how the boy, Kwai-Chang, got the nickname "Grasshopper." He is talking with Master Po in the garden and the blind priest tells him he must develop the ability to become so quiet that he can hear the grasshopper at his feet. Skeptical, the boy looks down and is surprised to see a grasshopper by his right foot.

He is amazed that the blind priest is aware the grasshopper is there.

He asks, "How is it, old man, that you can hear this grasshopper?"

The old priest smiles and answers, "How is it, young man, that you cannot?"

Jesus said, "Let anyone with ears to hear, listen!" (Luke 4:35 [NRSV])

Chapter Two
Follow Me!

When Jesus first began to gather his disciples he said to them simply, "Follow me."

"The next day Jesus decided to go to Galilee. When he got there, he ran across Philip and said, 'Come, follow me'" (John 1:43 [TMSG]).

To follow someone requires action, motion, change. We can't follow someone and yet stay where we are. We can't just read about a person's journey and be following that person. To follow we have to travel – we have to go along.

This is equally true of following Jesus. The disciples left their homes, their jobs and their families behind in order to go with Jesus. "Immediately, they left their father Zebedee, the boat, and the hired hands, and followed" (Mark 1:20 [TMSG]). "Then Peter chimed in, 'We left everything and followed you'" (Matthew 19:27 [TMSG]).

Following Jesus still requires leaving everything we know behind in order to live the abundant life he promises. This is vitally true in the psychological sense. You may know someone who constantly bemoans the fact that circumstances forced them to leave a city they loved, or a job, or a particular person. Psychologically they are clinging to the past and are unable to leave it behind.

Until they do they cannot fully embrace what life is offering them in the present. That's why Jesus teaches, "Anyone who puts a hand to the plow and then looks back is not fit for the Kingdom of God" (Luke 9:62 [NLT]).

True spiritual growth only occurs as we are psychologically willing to leave everything behind. This is one of the oldest teachings in the Bible. When we first meet Abraham in Genesis, God asks him to leave everything he knows behind and follow him into an unknown future. "Leave your country, your relatives, and your father's house, and go to the land that I will show you" (Genesis 12:1 [NLT]). Abraham's willingness to do this marks the beginning of his spiritual growth. This was true for Abraham and has been true for everyone since. That's why Jesus said, "What is born of the flesh is flesh, and what is born of the Spirit is spirit. . . . The wind blows where it chooses, and you hear the sound of it, but you do not know where it comes from or where it goes. So it is with everyone who is born of the Spirit" (John 3:6,8 [NRSV]). As long as we cling to what we already know – the flesh – we will remain stuck in the flesh, our present understanding. It is only when we are able to give up our psychological attachment to what we think we know that we can be born of the Spirit. Jesus even expressed amazement that Nicodemus could claim to be a spiritual teacher without understanding this fundamental truth. "Are you a teacher of Israel, and yet you do not understand these things?" (John 3:10 [NRSV])

Of course, Nicodemus was not alone. This human tendency to psychologically cling to what we think we know was also the biggest stumbling block for Jesus' disciples. Peter would often want to embrace the new possibilities Jesus offers but then allow his present understanding to hold him back. When he asked Jesus if he could come to him walking on the water, Jesus told him he could. And to his amazement he was able to do just that until he let what he thought he knew about the world stop him. "People can't walk on water!" Clinging to this belief Peter began to sink. "Jesus immediately reached out his hand and caught him, saying to him 'You of little faith, why did you doubt?'" (Matthew 14:31 [NRSV]) The disciples' failure to embrace the possibilities he offered them exasperated Jesus on more than one occasion, "You faithless and perverse generation, how much longer must I be with you? How much longer must I put with you?"(Matthew 17:17 [NRSV])

This human tendency to cling to the known is as old as time itself. When Adam and Eve ate from the Tree of the Knowledge of Good and Evil this knowledge created a barrier between them and God. Because of what they thought they knew, they hid from God. Prior to this they enjoyed open and trusting communion with God. They were willing to allow God to lead them. Afterwards, they were afraid of what might happen in the presence of God.

There is a profound saying in Alcoholics Anonymous that "If nothing changes, nothing changes." It is clear that if Jesus' vision of kingdom living is going to be realized in this world, if we are really going to leave everything we think we know behind and follow Jesus, we will have to change. And change is not easy, as we'll see. But it is worth it. In fact it is the only way to claim Jesus' promise to have life and have it abundantly.

Chapter 3
Wake Up!

Anthony DeMello has observed that most of us are walking around asleep. This was certainly true of a young man named Saul who lived in first century Jerusalem. He had been raised as a devout Jew, a Pharisee – one of the most pious sects in Judaism. He had studied with Gamaliel, one of the most prominent and respected rabbis of the day. And Saul was absolutely sure that he knew God's will for his people.

Saul was so content to live in the world of his ideas – what he thought he knew to be true – that he was unable to see what God was actually doing in the world. Saul was asleep, living in a dream world. So certain was he of his ideas about God and the world that he even consented to a lynching – the stoning of Stephen. He was determined to drive out this new heresy called "The Way."

"All this time Saul was breathing down the necks of the Master's disciples, out for the kill. He went to the Chief Priest and got arrest warrants to take to the meeting places in Damascus so that if he found anyone there belonging to the Way, whether men or women, he could arrest them and bring them to Jerusalem" (Acts 9:1-2 [TMSG]).

Saul was about to get the proverbial rude awakening: "When he got to the outskirts of Damascus, he was suddenly dazed by a blinding flash of light. As he fell to the ground, he heard a voice: 'Saul, Saul, why are you out to get me?' He said, 'Who are you, Master?' 'I am Jesus, the One you're hunting down. I want you to get up and enter the city. In the city you'll be told what to do next'" (Acts 9:3-6 [TMSG]).

In a flash, Saul's dream world was turned upside down. He who had been so confident now didn't know what to believe. What if everything he thought he knew was wrong? How would he live? How should he live? Saul was bewildered, dumbfounded. It was as though he was blind. "Saul, picking himself up off the ground, found himself stone blind. They had to take him by the hand and lead him into Damascus. He continued blind for three days. He ate nothing, drank nothing" (Acts 9:8-9 [TMSG]).

Jesus had to wake Saul up from his dream world so that he could enter into God's full world. Now, not knowing what else to do, he turned to God in prayer. "There was a disciple in Damascus by the name of Ananias. The Master spoke to him in a vision: 'Ananias.' 'Yes, Master?' he answered. 'Get up and go over to Straight Avenue. Ask at the house of Judas for a man from Tarsus. His name is Saul. He's there praying. He has just had a dream in which he saw a man named Ananias enter the house and lay hands on him so he could see again'" (Acts 9:10-12 [TMSG]).

Now that Saul could leave everything he thought he knew behind, he was free to follow Jesus and embrace the possibilities Jesus offered him. Jesus told Ananias, "I have picked him as my personal representative to Gentiles and kings and Jews" (Acts 9:15 [TMSG]). Saul woke up and became Paul, the apostle who wrote most of the New Testament and spread the good news of Jesus throughout the known world.

Jesus calls us, too, to wake up to the possibilities he offers us. Unfortunately, most of us don't want to wake up. Like Saul, we are content to live in our dream world. The world we create based on our past experience or the traditions that have been passed on to us. We dwell on past injustices (real or imagined) and tell ourselves that life's not fair. We dwell on past failures and tell ourselves, "I'll never amount to anything." We dwell on the shortcomings of others and tell ourselves, "You can't trust people. They'll just let you down."

Then in order to survive in such a dismal world we escape into an imaginary future. Like Saul, we think that all the world's problems will be solved if we can just get rid of that group of people who are ruining everything (followers of Jesus, communists, blacks, Muslims, MTV, or – (fill in the blank). Or, we think if I can just find the right person to marry then everything will be wonderful.

Or, if I can just get a divorce from this person (the one I used to think that marrying would solve all my problems) then everything will be ok. Or we tell ourselves that once the kids are grown and we retire then we will be able to enjoy life.

And so it goes. All day long we create an imaginary world based on the dead past or the imagined future and we completely miss God's full world that is all around us. Jesus calls us to wake up and discover the rich world of possibilities that God continually offers us – here and now. Jesus says, "Behold, the kingdom of God is within you" ([Luke 17:21 (KJV]).

Wake up! "Now is the right time to listen, the day to be helped. Don't put it off; don't frustrate God's work by showing up late" [2 Corinthians 6:2-3 (TMSG]).

Wake up!

Chapter 4
Look!

Jesus spent a good deal of his ministry encouraging people to wake up from their dream world, to let go of their preconceived ideas of how the world is, or how the world ought to be and **look** at the real world around them.

In his wonderful book, The Divine Conspiracy, Dallas Willard suggests that Jesus used a method of "show and tell" in his preaching to wake people up to God's full world. According to Matthew's gospel, right before preaching the Sermon on the Mount, Jesus is healing all who came to him. "Word got around the entire Roman province of Syria. People brought anybody with an ailment, whether mental, emotional, or physical. Jesus healed them, one and all" (Matthew 4:24 [TMSG]).

Then he leads the people up the hillside and begins to teach them. But what he teaches makes no sense in the world they know, nor I might add, does it make sense in the world most of us know. "You're blessed when you're at the end of your rope . . . You're blessed when you feel you've lost what is most dear to you." (Matthew 5:3-4 [TMSG]). "Blessed when you're at the end your rope?" "Blessed when you've lost what is most dear to you?" What in the world is Jesus talking about?

As Dallas Willard points out, Jesus has just healed those very people – those at the end of their rope, those who have lost everything dear to them. In other words those whose understanding of the world was that they had sinned and were being punished by God, or at the very least were not deserving of God's blessing. And yet, God had just visibly blessed them with healing through Jesus. Look!, says Jesus, in the real world your circumstances don't indicate your favor or disfavor with God, but God's blessing is available to you in the midst of your present circumstances, no matter what they are.

This is counter-intuitive. In Jesus' day people believed that those who were prosperous and healthy and successful were blessed by God and those who were poor and unhealthy and failures were not. Not much has changed in 2,000 years. Many people today still believe that some people are blessed by God and others are not.

We may believe, "I'm not worthy of God's blessing because I'm divorced." Or, "I'm not worthy of God's blessing because I'm fat." Or, "I'm not worthy of God's of blessing because I'm an alcoholic." Or, "I'm not worthy of God's blessing because I flunked out of school." Or, "I'm not worthy of God's blessing because I'm a bad person."

Our own or others' preconceived ideas of how we should be or shouldn't be convince us that we don't deserve God's blessing. This can happen to us at any age, but often it happens during childhood. Maybe we're told, "you're not good at math." Or maybe we're told, "you're too small to play football." Or maybe we're told, "people from our neighborhood don't go to college." Maybe we're told, "you'll never amount to anything." Too often we accept statements like these uncritically and allow them to shape our identity and self-understanding, thus limiting the possibilities we are able to accept for ourselves.

John Maxwell illustrates this beautifully in his book, The Winning Attitude, using the example of circus elephants. An elephant can easily pick up a one-ton load with his trunk. But, if you've ever visited the circus you may have watched these huge creatures standing quietly tied to a small wooden stake.

According to Maxwell, the trainers take a baby elephant while it is still young and weak and tie it by a heavy chain to an immovable iron stake. The elephant soon discovers that no matter how hard he tries, he cannot break the chain or move the stake. Then, no matter how large and strong the elephant becomes, he continues to believe he cannot move as long as he sees the stake in the ground beside him.

Unfortunately, many intelligent people act just like circus elephants. They let a bad or difficult experience limit their possibilities for the rest of their lives. They think they are unworthy of

God's blessing and deserve to live less than satisfactory lives. Jesus calls us to let go of the past and **look** at the real world in which God's blessing is available to all, if only we will accept it.

The Sermon on the Mount begins to make sense to us when we realize it is a call to let go of the dead past and the imagined future and look around at the real world, God's full world, in which we live. "You're blessed when you get your inside world – your mind and heart – put right. Then you can see God in the outside world" (Matthew 5:8 [TMSG]).

In the beatitudes and the well-known "You have heard it said . . . but I say to you passages" Jesus is basically telling us to wake up and **look** at what is really going on. We tell ourselves, "I'm not worthy of God's blessing because I can't seem to make my life work," but Jesus says to us, **Look,** "you're blessed when you're at the end of your rope." As the familiar poem, Footprints, reminds us, that is precisely when God carries us – when we are at the end of our rope and can't carry ourselves. God's blessing is available to us even in the midst of our poverty, our grief, and our inadequacies.

We may have been told all our lives and continue to tell ourselves, "You'll never amount to anything." Jesus says to us, **Look,** "you are the light of the world . . . let your light shine before others" (Matthew 5:14-16 [NRSV]).

We may have convinced ourselves that we have nothing worthwhile to contribute to life and to the world. Jesus tells us, **Look,** "you are the salt of the earth" (Matthew 5:13 [NRSV]). You add your own unique flavor to the world.

Jesus said, "You have heard that it was said to those of ancient times, 'You shall not murder'; and 'whoever murders shall be liable to judgment.' But I say to you that if you are angry with a brother or sister, you will be liable to judgment" (Matthew 5:21-22 [NRSV]).

Basically, Jesus is saying, "**Look!** Your anger pulls you out of the present moment, because the reason you are angry is that someone or something is not meeting your expectations of how people should behave or the way things ought to be." These expectations are based on ideas we have acquired from our parents, friends, teachers, etc., – in the past. As long as we are insisting on these expectations we are unable to really look at what is happening now.

In his immensely popular book, The Seven Habits of Highly Effective People, Steven Covey recalls a time when he rode the subway in New York City. A man boarded the subway car with his two young children. The children were running around the car creating havoc and disturbing the other passengers. The children were yelling back and forth, throwing things, even grabbing people's papers. Covey became increasingly irritated at the father's insensitivity and lack of discipline towards the children.

He confronted the man with the fact that his children were being very disruptive. The man responded that he knew he should probably do something but they were on their way home from the hospital where his wife, the children's mother had just died. He said, "I don't know what to think, and I guess they don't know how to handle it either." Covey commented that his whole perception of the situation was now different. "I saw things differently, and because I saw things differently, I thought differently, I felt differently, I behaved differently." He could now respond to the present situation rather than an imaginary situation created by his own preconceived ideas.

Jesus repeatedly calls us to **look** at the world the way it really is and to look into our hearts to understand what really is happening in our lives.

In other words, Jesus repeatedly advises us to become **aware**. This means we need to pay attention, not only to God's full world around us, but also to what is taking place within us. Otherwise our response to the circumstances and people in our lives will be inadequate because they are based on our preconceived ideas about ourselves and the world and not on what is really taking place. "Why do you see the speck in your neighbor's eye, but do not notice the log in your own eye? Or how can you say to your neighbor, 'Let me take the speck out of your eye,' while the log is in your own eye? You hypocrite, first take the log out of your own eye, and then you will see clearly to take the speck out of your neighbor's eye" (Matthew 7:3-5 [NRSV]).

Jesus calls us to become **aware** of preconceived ideas we have about ourselves and others so that we can then become **aware** of what is really taking place in God's full world. We can only do that in the present moment. Because, in reality, **now** is the only time there is. That's why Jesus makes a point of telling us to forget about the past and stop worrying about the future so that we can live fully in the present.

> "So I tell you, don't worry about everyday life – whether you have enough food, drink, and clothes. Doesn't life consist of more than food and clothing? Look at the birds. They don't need to plant or harvest or put food in barns because your heavenly Father feeds them. And you are far more valuable to him than they are. Can all your worries add a single moment to your life? Of course not. And why worry about your clothes? Look at the lilies and how they grow. They don't work or make their clothing, yet Solomon in all his glory was not dressed as beautifully as they are. And if God cares so wonderfully for flowers that are here today and gone tomorrow, won't he more surely care for you? You have so little faith!

So don't worry about having enough food or drink or clothing. Why be like the pagans who are so deeply concerned about these things? Your heavenly Father already knows all your needs, and he will give you all you need from day to day if you live for him and make the Kingdom of God your primary concern. So don't worry about tomorrow, for tomorrow will bring its own worries. Today's trouble is enough for today" (Matthew 6:25-34 [NLT]).

Jesus calls us to look around at what is taking place ***now***. Become aware of God's full world. If we want to experience the dynamic spirituality that Jesus offers, if we want to experience the abundant life, the eternal kind of life, we can only experience it ***now***. The psalmist reminds us that God is present every where and every when.

> Every moment you know where I am.
> You know what I am going to say
>   even before I say it, LORD.
> You both precede and follow me.
>   You place your hand of blessing on my head.
> Such knowledge is too wonderful for me,
>   too great for me to know!
> I can never escape from your spirit!
>   I can never get away from your presence!
>   Psalm 139:3-7 (NLT)

God is present here and now. All we have to do is wake up and **look** beyond the "log" in our eyes, our preoccupation with the past and the future, if we want to experience God's full world. Until we do so, we are spiritually blind as beautifully illustrated in John Newton's classic hymn, Amazing Grace, "I once was blind, but now I see."

Newton wrote that hymn when he realized that the world-view he had accepted was invalid. All his life he had believed that slavery was ok and even made his living as the captain of a slave-trading ship – until he became aware that the people he was helping sell into slavery were in reality spiritual beings, children of the living God, no less than he was. He woke up to his spiritual blindness and turned his life around.

This spiritual awakening, this becoming aware of God's full world is nothing less dramatic than Neo's waking up from the computer-generated dream world in the movie The Matrix. That's why Jesus calls it being "born again" or "born from above" (John 3:3). And it's why the apostle Paul, who as we saw in the last chapter ought to know, says of this awakening to God's full world, "What this means is that those who become Christians become new persons. They are not the same anymore, for the old life is gone. A new life has begun" (2 Corinthians 5:17 [NLT]).

A new life, real life in God's full world is waiting for us. All we have to do is take off our spiritual blinders and ***look***. "I once was blind, but now I see."

Chapter Five
Step Out!

No one likes change.

In his book, Developing the Leader Within You, John Maxwell relates the following story from Parables:

In the 1940s the Swiss watch was the most prestigious and best quality watch in the world. Consequently 80 percent of the watches sold in the world were made in Switzerland. In the late '50s the digital watch was presented to the leaders of the Swiss watch company. They rejected this new idea because they knew they already had the best watch and the best watchmakers. The man who had developed the digital watch subsequently sold the idea to Seiko.

In 1940 Swiss watch-making companies employed eighty thousand people. Today they employ eighteen thousand. In 1940, 80 percent of watches sold in the world were made in Switzerland. Today 80 percent of the watches are digital. This story represents what happens to many organizations and people: We choose to die rather than choose to change because change forces us out of our comfort zone.

Yet, if we want to live the abundant life, the eternal kind of life that Jesus offers us, we must change. Remember, if nothing changes, nothing changes.

At the end of the movie "Indiana Jones and the Last Crusade," Indy and his father have finally located the Holy Grail, which has been a life-long quest of Indy's father. Unfortunately, the Nazis have also found the secret location in the desert. In order to force Indy to solve three deadly riddles that are intended to keep the less-than-pure from reaching the grail, the Nazis shoot his father. Only the grail has the power to save him. The villain tells him, "It's time to decide what you really believe."

The last of the three deadly traps is a deep chasm that is too wide for anyone to leap over. Yet, Indy's father has drawn in his notebook a picture of a medieval knight walking across the chasm on thin air. Indy must decide whether to step out in faith or to let his father die. If he steps out and is wrong, he will fall to his death. There is no second chance. He takes a deep breath and steps forward. His foot lands on a stone bridge that has been polished to a mirror-like finish reflecting the walls of the canyon and causing the bridge to be invisible as one stands directly over it.

As we wake up and look around at the many and subtle ways we cling to what we know, or what we think we know about the world, we begin to realize that we are denying ourselves the abundant life Jesus offers. Still, it is all we know and we're not sure what it will be like to leave all that behind and follow Jesus. Like Indiana Jones stepping out in faith from the lion's head, we must ask ourselves what we really believe about Jesus. If we believe he is the Son of God surely we must take seriously what he taught. The same thing is true even if we believe that he was only a great teacher. He would not be a great teacher if what he taught has no real, practical value for every day living.

The problem, the secret that no one wants to admit, is this: the reason we don't believe it is that we've been taught all our lives, in a thousand subtle ways that it isn't true!

Jesus said, "Again I tell you, it is easier for a camel to go through the eye of a needle than for someone who is rich to enter the kingdom of God" (Matthew 19:24 [NRSV]).

We put bumper stickers on our cars that say, "The one with the most toys wins."

Jesus said, "you are to be perfect, even as your Father in heaven is perfect" (Matthew 5:48 [NLT]).

We say, "Nobody's perfect. We're only human. All we can do is the best we can."

Jesus said, "I assure you that everyone who has given up house or brothers or sisters or mother or father or children or property, for my sake and for the Good News, will receive now in return, a hundred times over, houses, brothers, sisters, mothers, children, and property" (Mark 10:29-30 [NLT]).

We tell our children, "Money doesn't grow on trees, you know."

Jesus said, "if anyone forces you to go one mile, go also the second mile" (Matthew 5:41 [NRSV]).

We tell ourselves, "If you give them an inch, they'll take a mile."

Jesus said, "if anyone strikes you on the right cheek, turn the other also" (Matthew 5:39 [NRSV]).

We say, "You've got to stand up for yourself. You can't be a door mat! People will walk all over you."

Jesus said, "You know that among the Gentiles those whom they recognize as their rulers lord it over them, and their great ones are tyrants over them. But it is not so among you; but whoever wishes to become great among you must be your servant" (Mark 10:42-43 [NRSV]).

Our culture says, "If you've got it, flaunt it. You deserve it, baby."

Everywhere we turn, we are bombarded with messages that contradict the teachings of Jesus. Is it any wonder that we don't believe him?

But, what if everything that Jesus taught is true? Wouldn't it make the most sense for us to actually apply his teachings in our lives in order to experience the eternal kind of life he talks about. "I assure you, those who listen to my message and believe in God who sent me have eternal life" (John 5:24 [NLT]). Eternal life begins **now** – if we can believe it. We don't have to wait until we die – Jesus invites us to begin living that kind of life even now.

Just as the piano teacher expects his or her students to learn how to actually play the piano, so Jesus expects his students to learn how to actually live the eternal kind of life beginning ***now***. ". . . the student who works hard will become like the teacher" (Luke 6:40 [NLT]). "The truth is, anyone who believes in me will do the same works I have done, and even greater works, because I am going to be with the Father. You can ask for anything in my name, and I will do it, because the work of the Son brings glory to the Father. Yes, ask anything in my name, and I will do it!" (John 14:12-14 [NLT])

Jesus said, "My purpose is to give life in all its fullness." (John 10:10 [NLT]). If we are ready to live life in all its fullness, Jesus is ready to give it to us right now. As Saul discovered on the road to Damascus, even though Jesus had been crucified and resurrected, Jesus is not absent from our world. On the contrary, he is our ever-present teacher and guide. "And be sure of this: I am with you always, even to the end of the age" (Matthew 28:20 [NLT]).

The question is, are we ready to take seriously Jesus' teaching, step out in faith and begin living life in all its fullness, the eternal kind of life? If not, we might as well close this book and go on believing whatever we want to believe. But, at least we can be honest with ourselves and admit what it is that we really believe.

Still, if our lives are not as peaceful, harmonious, loving, successful and meaningful as we'd like them to be; if we cannot honestly say with the apostle Paul, "I have learned how to get along happily whether I have much or little. I know how to live on almost nothing or with everything. I have learned the secret of living in every situation, whether it is with a full stomach or empty, with plenty or little. For I can do everything with the help of Christ who gives me the strength I need" (Philippians 4:11-13 [NLT]), then we may be ready to take seriously Jesus' teaching.

If so, we will have to abandon what we think we know and realize that we have been blind. "I have come to give sight to the blind and to show those who think they see that they are blind" (John 9:39 [NLT]). Then, we need to apply what Jesus teaches in our lives. As the apostle Paul put it, "Don't copy the behavior and customs of this world, but let God transform you into a new person by changing the way you think. Then you will know what God wants you to do, and you will know how good and pleasing and perfect his will really is" (Romans 12:2 [NLT]).

When we are ready to step out, we discover Jesus is there as he promised, ready to help us each step of the way. We discover that what he taught is trustworthy and true. "Anyone who listens to my teaching and obeys me is wise, like a person who builds a house on solid rock. Though the rain comes in torrents and the floodwaters rise and the winds beat against that house, it won't collapse, because it is built on rock. But anyone who hears my teaching and ignores it is foolish, like a person who builds a house on sand. When the rains and floods come and the winds beat against that house, it will fall with a mighty crash" (Matthew 7:24-27 [NLT]).

Jesus says, "Follow me." Are we ready to step out and follow him?

Chapter Six
Worship!

Jesus said, "'You must love the Lord your God with all your heart, all your soul, and all your mind.' This is the first and greatest commandment" (Matthew 22:37-38 [NLT]).

The abundant life begins with worship. We must be willing to put God first in our lives, to love God with all our heart, all our soul, and all our mind. We can only do that **now**, in the present moment. A little reflection on that statement will reveal that it is true of any relationship. It's like the farmer whose wife asked him if he loved her. He replied "Yes, when I stop to think about it."

Our goal is to think about God now, to see God in every moment and every activity of our lives. That is worship. True worship is loving God and placing God ahead of everything else in our lives.

Emmet Fox once wrote "When you love God more than you love your problem, you will be healed."

That statement really intrigued me when I first read it. What could he possibly mean by that? Then I remembered something that one of my seminary professors at the Claremont School of Theology, Dr. Kathy Black said in a lecture. She pointed out that the words healing and cure are not the same. Healing might include a cure, but it doesn't necessarily have to. Healing really means coming to a sense of peace, wholeness and well-being whether or not we are cured.

As I tried to get my mind around that, I realized it's possible to be cured and not healed. Plastic surgeon Maxwell Maltz, in his book, Psycho-Cybernetics, tells the story of a patient who came to him to have her nose fixed. She had a large nose that she thought made her look hideous. After her surgery, in which Dr. Maltz gave her a beautiful nose, she complained that he hadn't changed anything. To everyone else it was obvious that she had a new nose, but she still "saw" the old nose and considered herself hideous. She was "cured" but she wasn't healed.

Then I realized that it's also possible to be healed and not cured. At a former church, I had a friend who only has one arm. On the other he has a prosthesis with a clamp that serves as an artificial hand. I remember quite vividly my friend patiently and gently showing our three small children his artificial arm. He showed them how he could flex this muscle and bend the artificial elbow; flex another muscle and operate the clamp that served as his hand on that arm. He is at peace with his condition. He is healed but not cured. He hasn't grown a new arm.

Now, back to Emmet Fox's statement, "When you love God more than you love your problem you will be healed." We tend to think that our problems are what is keeping us from loving God. We may tell ourselves, "How can I love God when he allowed this to happen to me?" Or we may tell ourselves, "Of course I want to love God, but I have to take care this before I can give the time to daily devotionals or take time to get involved in church." Or, we may tell ourselves, "That's crazy! Who would love their problems more than they love God? I don't love my problem! Why doesn't God take away my problem and then I'll be able to spend more time with God."

The truth is, our problem is not our problem. Our problem whatever it is, doesn't keep us from loving God. There are other people with the same problem who are healed – maybe not cured – but they have a sense of peace, wholeness and well-being. If our problem is not our problem then what is our problem?

Our problem is we don't love God with all our heart, with all our soul and with all our mind. We don't put God first in our lives. As crazy as it sounds, we love our problems more than we love God. We spend more time thinking about our problems than we do about God.

I have always been a champion pouter. When I'm upset about something I go into a funk and sulk. And I pout. I can do this for hours. I can do this for days. Now here's the really weird part – even when I realize that I'm pouting and even when I realize that I can turn to God in prayer and God will help me through it. Even when I realize that God will turn me around if I only ask. Even though I know all of that, I refuse to do it. Most of the time it's because I'm afraid that God is going to ask me to do something I don't want to do – like apologize to someone. Or ask forgiveness from someone. Or even worse, to forgive someone!

In other words, I'm afraid that God is going to ask me to love Him more than I love my problem. But, I have learned that when I do finally turn to God, I am healed.

When we love God more than we love our problem, we are healed.

Jesus says the greatest commandment of all is to love God with all our heart, and with all our soul, and with all our mind. Whatever we think is our problem, is not really our problem. The problem is we're not loving God with all of our heart, with all of our soul, and with all of our mind. In fact, that's the only real problem we have.

When we focus on our problems, we are either rehearsing something that as happened to us (how could God let this happen?) or we are anticipating an imaginary future (what will I do if this happens?). Either way, in our minds we are living in the dead past or an imaginary future which prevents us from loving God because it is only possible to love someone, really love someone, in the present moment. Now is the only time there is. We can't love someone one hour from now. We can't love someone one hour ago. Now is the only time we ever have. Everything happens now.

As Paul writes to the Romans, "To set the mind on the flesh (the dead past or imaginary future) is death, but to set the mind on the Spirit is life and peace" (Romans 8:6 [NRSV]). When we dwell on our problems, we are setting our mind on the flesh. When we love God with all that we are, we are setting our mind on the Spirit.

Whenever we find ourselves dwelling on events that have already happened or worrying about future events that may or may not ever happen, we need to bring our minds back to the present moment. Look closely, attentively at what is actually happening right now. This takes tremendous discipline, but if we love God enough to do it, if we love God with all our heart, with all our soul and with all our mind, right now and every now, then we are truly living in the present moment, then we are healed. We find a sense of well-being – of life and peace – and we begin to understand how much God loves us. Then we want to please God. Now. Out of the love we feel for God we want to contribute to God's happiness. Now. We want to be a part of what God is doing in the world right now. We want to use the spiritual gifts that God gives us to help God accomplish God's plans. And we experience the fruits of the Spirit in our daily lives: love, joy, peace, patience, kindness, goodness, faithfulness, gentleness.

Don't say this is all too simple; it sounds too good to be true. Don't be obstinate, but try it. Your willingness to try it by becoming aware of the present moment, what is actually happening right now, is the "faith as small as a mustard seed" that Jesus talks about: "I assure you, even if you had faith as small as a mustard seed you could say to this mountain, 'Move from here to there,' and it would move. Nothing would be impossible" (Matthew 17:20 [NLT]).

Remember, Jesus continually calls us to **wake up** and **look** at what is actually happening right now. "I am telling you to stop worrying about your life . . . But first be concerned about God's kingdom and his righteousness, and all of these things will be provided for you as well. So never worry about tomorrow, for tomorrow will worry about itself" (Matthew 6:25, 33-34 [ISVNT]). Don't worry about the future, one minute from now, one day from now, one week from now or one year from now. If you want to affect what will happen in the future, you can only do it now. Let go of the past, there's nothing you can do to change it. Now is the only time you can do anything. "Anyone who puts a hand to the plow and then looks back is not fit for the Kingdom of God." Now is the only time there is.

"Have faith in God! Truly I tell you, if anyone says to this mountain, 'Be lifted up and thrown into the sea,' if he doesn't doubt in his heart but believes that what he says will happen, it will be done for him. That is why I tell you, whatever you ask for in prayer, believe that you have received it and it will be yours" (Mark 11:22-24 [ISVNT]).

Be here now. The only place you can ever meet God is here. The only time you can ever meet God is now. "Be still, and know that I am God" (Psalm 46:10 [NRSV]). Worship God by loving God with all your heart, all your soul and all your mind right now. The eternal kind of life is here right now. "For, in fact, the kingdom of God is among you" (Luke 17:21 [NRSV]).

Chapter Seven
Care!

As we begin to love God with all our heart, all our soul, all our mind and all our strength, we begin to experience God's presence with us in each moment. We discover that "indeed he is not far from each one of us. For 'In him we live and move and have our being'" (Acts 17:27-28 [NRSV]). God becomes our constant companion, walking beside us, guiding us and protecting us. "The LORD is my shepherd" (Psalm 23:1 [NRSV]). Our hearts are filled with love for all of God's creation for we see God's hand everywhere. We recognize that other people are also children of God and our brothers and sisters.

Until we put God first in our life, love God with all our heart, soul, mind and strength, we cannot really love other people. Once we put God first then we cannot help but see others as children of God. Then we discover what it really means to love them as well. Loving others becomes one of the ways we love God here and now. In addition to the greatest commandment, to love God with all our heart, soul, mind and strength, Jesus teaches us, "A second is equally important: 'Love your neighbor as yourself'" (Matthew 22:39 [NLT]).

Just as we can only love God here and now, we can only love our neighbors here and now. In fact, when we are truly present with someone here and now, we can't help but love them, because we see them as children of God, created in God's image. We see Christ in them. "Truly I tell you, just as you did it to one of the least of these who are members of my family, you did it to me" (Matthew 25:40 [NRSV]).

The problem is that just as we are not always present for God here and now, we are not always present for our neighbors here and now. As human beings we have been blessed with the wonderful ability to "know." We have the capacity to learn and store and use information. For example, we can learn that two plus two equals four. And we can then store that information in our memory and know that we know that two plus two equals four. That information becomes useful to me if my wife and I invite another couple over for dinner we can easily determine how many places settings we need on the table.

This ability to know that we know is unique to human beings and has allowed us to develop electric lights, movies, television and even send people to the moon and bring them back safely. It is a wonderful tool when it is used appropriately. Just as morphine is a wonderful tool for managing pain when it is used appropriately. But when morphine is abused, it becomes addictive and creates a distorted version of reality that dominates our view of reality.

The same thing can be true of our ability to "know that we know." That's because sometimes we think we know something when we don't. If we aren't paying attention, this is a byproduct of the way we relate to the world and just like a drug addiction it can lead to a distorted view of reality

You see, as human beings, we are constantly cataloguing the world around us as we encounter it. We see a car and immediately, our mind searches our database until we find a match for that car, say a Cadillac Seville. If we've never seen a Cadillac Seville before then we may examine the car and build our database of information so that the next time we see one we will know immediately what it is.

We also do this when we meet other people. Let's say you and I meet at a party. The first thing we try to do is get enough information about each other so that we can find each other in our database. You learn that I'm a minister and if you've had pleasant experiences with ministers, seen them as role models, spiritual guides, compassionate, caring, etc. – you might think to yourself, "cool." On the other hand, if you've had negative experiences with ministers, seen them as judgmental, condemning, hell, fire and brimstone types, you might think, "well I'll find someone else to talk to at this party."

That's all fine as far as it goes, but the problem is your idea of who I am based on your perception of ministers may or may not coincide with the reality of who I am. For example, if you are someone who puts ministers up on a pedestal, sees them as especially righteous and holy, just maybe a half-step removed from God and I tell you a slightly off-color joke at the party, you may be shocked, disappointed and think, "How could someone who is a man of God say such a thing." Well, the truth is, pastors are people, too, and we're not any more perfect or righteous or holy than anyone else.

What gets us into trouble is that sometimes my idea of you is what has a relationship with your idea of me, and the real you and the real me have no relationship at all, but we think we do. We may begin with a genuine relationship, but then we catalogue each other and over time we fail to notice how the other person may be growing or changing. And this makes it very hard for either of us to change because the other keeps forcing us back into their idea of who we are.

Tony Campolo tells a wonderful story about the time a friend of his counseled a man who was falling out of love with his wife. Tony's friend advised the man to think of all the ways he could make life happier for his wife and then do them. A few days later Tony's friend received a phone call in which the husband related the following:

"Every day I leave for work, put in a hard day, come home dirty and sweaty, stumble in the back door, go to the refrigerator, get something to drink, and then go into the rec room and watch television until supper time. After talking to you, I decided I would do better than that in the future. So yesterday, before I left work, I showered and shaved and put on a clean shirt. On the way home I stopped at the florist and bought a bouquet of roses. Instead of going in the back door as I usually do, I went to the front door and rang the doorbell. My wife opened the door, took one look at me, and started to cry.

"When I asked her what was wrong she said, 'It's been a horrible day. First Billy broke his leg and had to have it put in a cast. I no sooner returned home from the hospital and your mother called and told me that she is coming to stay for three weeks. I tried to do the wash and the washing machine broke and there is water all over the basement. And now you have to come home drunk!'"

The housewife was relating to her idea of her husband and couldn't see who he was becoming in that moment. Like that housewife, we tend to see the world not as the world is, but as we have learned to see the world. We learn this as we are growing up from our parents, siblings, teachers, churches, government, television, movies, music, etc. We catalogue our world based on this information and that is how we relate to the world. This is what psychologists call our conditioning. Again, it is a wonderful tool when used appropriately, but when it is abused it creates a distorted version of reality that keeps us from loving our neighbor here and now by preventing us from really seeing them as they are right now.

Our conditioning is the log in our eye that Jesus talks about: "Why worry about a speck in your friend's eye when you have a log in your own? How can you think of saying, 'Let me help you get rid of that speck in your eye,' when you can't see past the log in your own eye? Hypocrite! First get rid of the log from your own eye; then perhaps you will see well enough to deal with the speck in your friend's eye" (Matthew 7:3-5 [NLT]).

The way to remove the log from our eye is to be come aware, to pay attention to what is happening right now, in the present moment. The instant we allow our minds to drift into the past, to what we think we know about the person or to what we have learned from our culture about how someone ought to behave, – in that instant we are blinded by the log of our conditioning. We need to return to the here and now. We need to ask ourselves "what is really happening right here, right now?" We need to listen to the other and see through our conditioning to see them as they really are. Only then can we love them.

When you are with another person, be fully present with them now. Look at them as though you were seeing them for the first time. Look into their eyes. Hear the quality of their voice. See the presence of Christ in them and pay attention to what they are saying and doing. Love God and love your neighbor as yourself. Here and now. That is the only time you will ever have to do it.

Jesus said, "So now I am giving you a new commandment: Love each other. Just as I have loved you, you should love each other. Your love for one another will prove to the world that you are my disciples" (John 13:34-35 [NLT]).

Chapter Eight
Be Perfect!

"God created people in his own image; God patterned them after himself; male and female he created them" (Genesis 1:27 [NLT]). We are spiritual beings, "For God is Spirit" (John 4:24 [NLT]) and we are created in the image of God. As we put God first in our lives – as we love God with all of our heart, soul, mind and strength in each present moment, our spirituality awakens and begins to develop. We discover that we are living in another dimension, the kingdom of God. We discover that the spiritual life is life. Until then we are, as Rick Warren puts it, "just marking time."

We can never really be fulfilled, loving, content, and peaceful until we are living from the reality that we are spiritual beings, children of the living God. Jesus said, "In a word, what I'm saying is, Grow up. You're kingdom subjects. Now live like it. Live out your God-created identity" (Matthew 5:48 [TMSG]). The time to do that is now. "Listen, now is the 'right time'! Now is the 'day of salvation'!" (2 Corinthians 6:2 [ISVNT]).

The way life works is like this: Each and every moment we have the ability to choose how we are going to live right now. We can't choose how we are going to live yesterday, or how we are going to live tomorrow. We can choose right now to make plans for tomorrow, but when it comes time to execute those plans, it will be now.

As we choose how to live each moment, we are influenced by many voices: the voices of our parents as we were growing up, the voices of our teachers, our minister, our friends, our own past experience (remember when I tried that – boy that was a mistake) as well as politicians, celebrities, song writers, authors, advertisers, etc; all giving us advice on how to live, or telling us what is normal and to be expected in life. As we make our decision, we often accept one of these suggestions from the many voices that influence us. These voices may come from our past conditioning, the present (someone may be in the room with us right now telling us what we should do) or the imagined future (if I do this so-and-so will get mad at me). As we incorporate our choice for each moment in to our lives, we determine what our lives will be like.

We are creatures of habit and the more we choose a particular way of being in the world, the easier it is to choose the same way again – even if that way doesn't work all that well. So we may continue to go to the casino and gamble even though we know it is cleaning out our bank account. Or we may continue to drink every night even though it has destroyed our relationships and our career. Or we may continue to get involved in relationship after relationship with persons that take advantage of us or abuse us. Or we may continue to drift from one unsatisfying job to another. Or we may continue to alienate our children or our parents by the way we habitually treat them. We find ourselves in the proverbial vicious cycle.

There is a way out. As we make our decision in each moment about how to live our lives, there is another voice that offers to influence us – the "still, small voice" of God (1 Kings 19:12 [KJV]). In each moment God offers us the possibility that will lead to the greatest benefit and growth in our lives. This is why it is so important to live in the present moment, here and now. Now is the only time we can tune into God's wisdom and draw on his advice. In order to tune in to God's possibility for us we remove our attention from all the other voices that seek to influence us and turn our attention towards God. Jesus said, "The way to life – to God! – is vigorous and requires total attention" (Matthew 7:14 [TMSG]).

This means, as Jesus says in Matthew 5:48, we need to grow up. Growing up simply means taking responsibility for our own lives rather than constantly looking to some other person or persons to tell us how to live and what to do. Growing up means we recognize that the reason our life isn't working as well as we'd like is because of the choices we make. This recognition allows us to break the cycle of habit and make new choices, just as the alcoholic's recognition that s/he has a drinking problem is the first step in breaking that cycle.

Unfortunately, almost no one wants to grow up. Growing up, taking responsibility for our lives means we have to give up being a victim. If we take responsibility for our lives we can no longer blame things on some one else. We can no longer say things like, "I need to drink because my job sucks and it's the only way I can cope with it." Or, "I need to have affairs outside of marriage because my wife doesn't understand me." Or, "I can't do my job properly because my boss is a jerk." Or, "I can't get a better job because I don't have a college degree." Or, "My life sucks because _____ ." Growing up means we have to admit to ourselves that at least one of the reasons our life isn't working as well as we'd like, is because of the choices we make, and the choices we make have consequences. Once we realize that we are responsible for the choices we make, we realize that we can make different choices.

Perhaps this is one reason why Jesus says, "I assure you, unless you turn from your sins (the choices we've made that carry the consequences we don't like) and become as little children, you will never get into the Kingdom of Heaven" (Matthew 18:3 [NLT]). Most children I have known can't wait to grow up. They want to be able to make their own decisions about life. We need to recapture that spirit and open ourselves to perceive and choose the possibilities that God offers us in each moment.

The New Revised Standard Version translates Jesus' statement in Matthew 5:48 as "Be perfect, therefore, as your heavenly Father is perfect." Notice that Jesus says we are to " be perfect" – now. Not "you will be perfect" or "you might be perfect" or "you will become perfect". No, we are to "be perfect" here and now. If we believe that Jesus knows what he is talking about, then it must be possible for us to be perfect now.

In fact, that is the only time we can ever be perfect, because that is the only time we can experience God and tune into God's perfect possibility for us. Instead of tuning into God right now, we create time in our minds, psychological time. We tell ourselves, "I don't have time to devote to God right now, I'll do it when the kids start school." Then, we tell ourselves, "I'm too busy taxiing the kids to school and all of their activities, I'll have time for God once the kids leave home." Then we tell ourselves, "I'm too tired after work and helping with my grandchildren, I'll have time for God once I retire."

And so it goes. We create a mythical time in our minds when we are going to connect to God. Since that mythical time never arrives or when it does arrive it is superseded by another mythical time, we never seem to connect with God.

Another psychological tendency that prevents us from connecting with God is that we try to do too many things at once in our mind. In reality, we can only do one thing at a time. But, we start thinking about all of the things we have to get done today and psychologically we create pressure on ourselves to get them all accomplished right now. As we allow this pressure to build in ourselves, we create stress. If the stress becomes too great, we may flit from one activity to another trying to relieve the pressure so that nothing really gets done well.

This tendency carries over into our minds when we hear a statement like "be perfect as your heavenly Father is perfect." In our minds, we create scenario after scenario that we perceive as being too difficult for us to respond to perfectly. And, in our minds we create the illusion that "be perfect" means we have deal with all of those situations right now and that thought is too overwhelming "I can't be perfect! After all, I'm not Jesus. I'm not God. I'm only human." And so we create a mythical time in our minds, probably when we get to heaven, when God is somehow going to change us so that we can be perfect.

But, Jesus says it is possible right now to "be perfect as your heavenly Father is perfect." How do we do that? Alcoholics Anonymous has learned the secret and applied it very effectively in their treatment of alcoholics. If the alcoholic concentrates on trying to quit drinking forever, it is too much. The thought of never being able to have another drink is too overwhelming. So they concentrate on "one day at a time." This gives them freedom to make a choice. They can choose, "I don't have to drink today. I can go one day without a drink."

The key to following Jesus admonition to "be perfect" is to bring that focus down to the present moment. Even the thought of having to be perfect all day can be overwhelming. Fortunately, we don't have to think that way. Each moment we can choose how we're going to conduct our lives. Right now I can keep on doing what I've always done or I can do something different. I can continue to run on auto-pilot, allowing the momentum of my habits, my past choices to propel me forward. Or, I can turn to God and ask for guidance. I can open myself to the possibilities that God offers me.

Right now we can choose to do what God would have us do, or we can listen to the other voices in the world that seek to influence our lives. Right now, we can choose to gossip about our neighbor or we can choose to wait until later to talk about that. Right now we can choose to tell the boss where to go, or we can choose to wait on that. Right now we can choose to think about God, or we can choose to think about what we're going to do this evening or what happened to us yesterday. In reality, we do make such choices every moment. The trouble is that most of time we do it unconsciously. Jesus calls us to wake up and make our choices consciously, "The way to life – to God! – is vigorous and requires total attention" (Matthew 7:14 [TMSG]).

As we begin to choose God's possibility for our lives right now, our lives begin to work better. "Then you will know what God wants you to do, and you will know how good and pleasing and perfect his will really is" (Romans 12:2). The more we choose God's possibility for us in the present moment the easier it becomes to choose God's possibility in the next present moment. We grow in our ability to live the spiritual life. Then we are really living. As we watch our lives improve we realize what Paul means by "work out your own salvation with fear and trembling; for it is God who is at work in you, enabling you both to will and to work for his good pleasure" (Philippians 2:12-13 [NRSV]).

"Give your entire attention to what God is doing now, and don't get worked about what may or may not happen tomorrow. God will help you deal with whatever hard things come up when the time comes" (Matthew 6:34 [TMSG]). Ancient wisdom states it beautifully, "yesterday is but a dream and tomorrow is but a vision. But today well-lived makes every yesterday a dream of happiness and every tomorrow a vision of hope" (Anonymous).

Chapter Nine
Practice!

Our willingness to believe that Jesus knows what he is talking about and apply it in our lives is the faith the size of a mustard seed that allows us to enter another dimension of living – the Kingdom of God. Jesus uses the illustration of the mustard tree to describe how this small beginning blossoms into eternal life. "It is like a tiny mustard seed. Though this is one of the smallest of seeds, it grows to become one of the largest of plants, with long branches where birds can come and find shelter" (Mark 4:31-32 [NLT]).

Like the mustard seed, our faith, our confidence in Jesus that his teaching is true, gives birth to our spirituality so that we can live in the Kingdom of God and be perfect as our heavenly Father is perfect. We have seen that the key is to live in the present moment, the eternal now. This sounds very simple and it is, but it is not always easy to do. Especially when we are very upset or preoccupied with the events and circumstances of our lives. Our spirituality is like a muscle that can be developed and strengthened. Living fully in the present moment is a skill which improves with practice much like playing the piano or throwing a football.

The famous classical pianist Artur Rubenstein once said of his daily piano practice that "if I miss one day, I know it, two days, my friends know it, and three days the whole world knows it."

Just as it is important to practice the piano, it is important to practice living fully in the eternal now. The fifteenth century monk Brother Lawrence called this Practicing the Presence of God. We practice seeing the presence of God everywhere for we know that we can never get away from God's presence for God is everywhere (Psalm 139). If we feel distant or removed from God, if we are not aware of God's presence with us in this moment it is because we have moved. And we can only move away from God in our minds, since in reality God is everywhere whether we are aware of it or not. "Or don't you know that your body is the temple of the Holy Spirit, who lives in you and was given to you by God" (1 Corinthians 6:19 [NLT]).

If we can only be separated from God in our minds, then the key to experiencing God here and now is to turn our minds towards God. We do this by reminding ourselves of what we know about God whenever we catch our minds wandering to the dead past or the imagined future. Instead of worrying about mistakes we have made or wrongs that have been committed against us or worrying about what we're going to do about this problem or that problem that may happen in the future, we remind ourselves that God is with us. We remind ourselves that God is all-powerful; that God is love; that God is everywhere present; that God is wisdom and intelligence; and that God is in us for we are temples of the Holy Spirit.

It is easier for us to practice the presence of God and develop our spirituality with other people of who are on a spiritual path. "God said, 'It is not good for the man to be alone'" (Genesis 2:18 [TMSG]).

This is so because the nature of the universe is relationship. All things that exist are in relationship. The science of quantum physics has discovered that an observer and the system being observed are mysteriously linked so that the results of any observation seemed to be determined in part by actual choices made by the observer. The observer affects the observed. In other words, what I do potentially affects you and everything else in the world and what you do potentially affects me and everything else in the world. This is illustrated by Edward Lorenz's theory of "the butterfly effect" which suggests that the flapping of a butterfly's wings in one area of the world may cause such a disturbance in the atmosphere that it results in a tornado in another part of the world.

Our relationship with others not only affects them, it affects us in ways that science is just beginning to understand. Dr. Stephanie Brown, a psychologist at the University of Michigan in Ann Arbor conducted a five year study of altruism – providing social support for others. Her study showed that older people who reported helping someone else just once a year were likely to live longer, as were husbands and wives who were able to make their spouse feel loved and cared for.

Those who were closest to Jesus, the disciples and the first community of believers, understood this principle very well. Paul's favorite illustration of this truth is the "Body of Christ" in which he points out that all the parts of a body work together to promote the health of the whole body (Romans 12). Just as a finger or a toe or a kidney cannot survive in isolation, so too, followers of Jesus need one another to promote each other's spiritual health.

Peter encourages us to "Come to him, a living stone, though rejected by mortals yet chosen and precious in God's sight, and like living stones, let yourselves be built into a spiritual house" (1 Peter 2:4-5 [NRSV]). Again, all of the stones promote and support the strength of the house.

In a community of believers we can share our struggles with living in the presence of God here and now. We can share what distractions pull our minds away from the now and learn from others how they manage to remain centered in those situations. We can also share with them how we remain centered in the situations that tend to pull us out of the present moment.

With other believers we can re-visit the teaching of Jesus and the early believers to hold each other accountable for really accepting Jesus' teaching as true and applying it in our lives. (Are we really "walking our talk.")

The early believers really understood the benefits of sharing their spiritual journeys together and their daily lives were a powerful testimony to how effective this practice was. "And all the believers met together constantly and shared everything they had. They sold their possessions and shared the proceeds with those in need. They worshiped together at the Temple each day, met in homes for the Lord's Supper, and shared their meals with great joy and generosity—all the while praising God and enjoying the goodwill of all the people. And each day the Lord added to their group" (Acts 2:44-47 [NLT]).

They understood that the intent of Jesus' teaching is to give us sound advice on how to live happily and effectively. They understood that Jesus meant it when he said the way to life is to love God with all our heart, all our soul, all our mind and all our strength; and to love our neighbor as ourselves. They understood that his new commandment to love one another can only be carried out in community.

More deeply than that, they understood that through their love for their neighbors, they were, in fact, really loving God, for each of them was a temple for the Holy Spirit. They understood that Jesus meant what he said when he promised them, "For where two or three are gathered in my name, I am there among them" (Matthew 18:20 [NRSV]).

The spiritual life is lived most effectively in community with others who take the spirituality and the teachings of Jesus seriously. On the night before his death, Jesus embarrassed his disciples by kneeling down and washing their feet. Afterwards, he said to them, ""Do you understand what I was doing? You call me 'teacher' and 'Lord,' and you are right, because it is true. And since I, the Lord and Teacher, have washed your feet, you ought to wash each other's feet. I have given you an example to follow. Do as I have done to you. How true it is that a servant is not greater than the master. Nor are messengers more important than the one who sends them. You know these things—now do them! That is the path of blessing" (John 13:12-17 [NLT]).

The blessing doesn't come in knowing what Jesus taught. The blessing comes from applying what Jesus taught in our every day lives. As Jesus said, "Knowing the correct password – saying 'Master, Master,' for instance – isn't going to get you anywhere with me. What is required is serious obedience – doing what my Father wills" (Matthew 7:21 [TMSG]).

Try it. Accept the abundant life Christ offers you – live the life for which you were created and see if you don't find yourself part of a living, caring and loving community through which people powerfully experience Christ's love and presence here and now.

Chapter Ten
Share!

As our spirituality grows it becomes easier and easier for us to see the presence of God with us in each moment here and now. As our spiritual understanding grows we realize that the abundant life is found in giving ourselves away to others. Jesus said, "For those who want to save their life will lose it, and those who lose their life for my sake, and for the sake of the gospel, will save it. For what will it profit them to gain the whole world and forfeit their life?" (Mark 8:35-36 [NRSV]) God wants to bless us abundantly so that we can be a blessing to others. "Don't be afraid of missing out. You're my dearest friends! The Father wants to give you the very kingdom itself. Be generous. Give to the poor. Get yourselves a bank that can't go bankrupt, a bank in heaven far from bank robbers, safe from embezzlers, a bank you can count on" (Luke 12:32-33 [TMSG]).

Jesus spoke more about our relationship to our property and our money than he did on any other single topic. That's because Jesus understood that our relationship to our money is one of the most powerful indicators we have of how well we are doing at living in the presence of God in the eternal now, which is the only time we can ever live in the awareness of God's presence. Our relationship to money is a powerful tool we can use to gage whether we are loving God with all our heart, all our soul, all our mind and all our strength. Jesus said, "Wherever your treasure is, there your heart and thoughts will also be" (Matthew 6:21 [NLT]). If we really want to know where our heart is, all we have to do is read through our check register and see where our treasure goes.

When we are truly living in the conscious awareness of God's presence with us right now, we realize that our money and our property belong to God already and he has lovingly provided them for us to use for our benefit and the benefit others. "The earth is the LORD'S, and everything in it. The world and all its people belong to him" (Psalm 24:1 [NLT]).

The problem is, instead of living in the present moment with God we create psychological time in our minds. We worry about how we will pay the bills tomorrow if we give our money to God today. We think about things we would like to be able to do but cost money. If we give our money to God then we won't have enough to do the things we want. As we worry about these things our minds are no longer in the present moment with God.

This is certainly what happened to me. I had read about the spiritual benefits of tithing (giving ten percent of our income to God – Deuteronomy 12:6 [NRSV]). I was aware of God's promises to bless us more than we can imagine if we do so. God even challenges us to test him on this promise: "Bring your full tithe to the Temple treasury so there will be ample provisions in my Temple. Test me in this and see if I don't open up heaven itself to you and pour out blessings beyond your wildest dreams" (Malachi 3:10 [TMSG]).

I knew of all of this and I wanted to tithe. I wanted to give ten percent of my income to God. But, I created psychological time in mind. I reasoned that I couldn't afford to give ten percent right now, but as soon as I made enough money I would start to do so. In other words, I created a mythical time in my mind when I would be able to afford to give ten percent to God. In my mind I pretended that I was honoring God with the amount I was giving to God because I intended to give more sometime. Instead of trusting God here and now, I tried to bargain with God: "God, as soon as you give me the income, I will tithe on it."

I didn't realize what I was doing at the time, but I was living in an imaginary future where I could give my heart to God instead of giving God my heart now.

About that time I met my wife Candace and we got married. The first Sunday after our wedding we had to write the check for the church offering. I told Candace that we ought to talk about what would be a reasonable offering to make – based on our newly combined income. She told me ten percent would do quite nicely. She had tithed all her life and saw no reason to change now.

As you can imagine, I had a little trouble breathing at that moment. Ten percent! She couldn't be serious – we had three kids to support. We had a big house payment. Three kids. A car payment. Three kids. But the words of Malachi came back to me, "Put me to the test, says the Lord of hosts" (Malachi 3:10 [NRSV]). So, I swallowed the lump in my throat and wrote the check for ten percent of our income. And we have been tithing ever since.

And God has been true to God's word. The heavens have been opened to give us blessing upon blessing. Now, I must caution you – these were not necessarily financial blessings, though some have been. We are not independently wealthy. In fact, there have been many weeks when we sweated out where the money was going to come from to meet our financial obligations. But, the money always arrives. As Lloyd Olgivie once said, "God is never late, but he is rarely early." We have never lacked for anything that we needed.

But, the real blessing that has come is in my relationship with God and my own spiritual development, as Jesus well understood. I have learned to trust God and to turn to God in times of need. And God is always there. And the frosting on the cake is the joy we get from giving to God. I used to worry all the time that the church would ask me for more money. I used to worry that I wouldn't have enough or I wouldn't be able to make my pledge. Once I began tithing, began giving ten percent of my income to God, this was no longer an issue. God has promised that if I will do my part, God will do God's part. "Put me to the test, says the Lord of Hosts."

Having said that, it is important to note that the key is not to give in order to receive God's blessing or in order to get more stuff – money, property, etc. The key is to get our hearts right with God, to live fully in the conscious awareness of God's presence right here and right now. When we do that we will want to give back because we love God with all our heart, all our soul, all our mind and all our strength. We love God with everything we have, including or financial resources.

Paul well understood this principle that we have a loving and generous God who blesses us abundantly so that we can bless others. "God loves it when the giver delights in the giving. God can pour on the blessings in astonishing ways so that you're ready for anything and everything, more than just ready to do what needs to be done. As one psalmist puts it, He throws caution to the winds, giving to the needy in reckless abandon. His right-living, right-giving ways never run out, never wear out. This most generous God who gives seed to the farmer that becomes bread for your meals is more than extravagant with you. He gives you something you can then give away, which grows into full-formed lives, robust in God" (2 Corinthians 9:7-10 [TMSG]).

The more we receive, the more we have available to share with others, here and now. Jesus said, "From everyone to whom much has been given, much will be required; and from the one to whom much has been entrusted, even more will be demanded" (Luke 12:48 [NRSV]).

Chapter Eleven
Go!

"The way to life – to God! – is vigorous and requires total attention" (Matthew 7:14 [TMSG]) for the habit of creating psychological time is deeply entrenched in us. Even after the disciples had been with Jesus for three years, had learned the lessons of abundant living at his feet and practiced what he taught and had witnessed his triumph over death – his resurrection – they still lapsed into the habit of creating psychological time. Right before his ascension to heaven, they asked him when he was going to change everything and make it right. In other words they asked about an imagined future. They still had a tendency to focus on some time in the future that does not yet exist, rather than live in the eternal now.

Jesus then reminded them that they were asking the wrong question. "It is not for you to know the times or periods that the Father has set by his own authority" (Acts 1:6 [NRSV]). They should have been asking "how are we to live now?" "What is God asking us to do now?" Jesus told them they were to wait expectantly for power from the Holy Spirit when they would "be my witnesses in Jerusalem, in all Judea and Samaria, and to the ends of the earth" (Acts 1:8 [NRSV]).

To wait expectantly does not mean to do nothing. Rather it means to practice the presence of God here and now, to pay attention so we don't miss the possibilities, the power, that God offers us in each moment. This is why right after this the disciples were "constantly devoting themselves to prayer" (Acts 1:14 [NRSV]). They were tuning into God's presence with them in the present moment.

As we develop our conscious awareness of God's presence in the present moment, we experience the eternal, abundant kind of life Jesus talks about. And once we experience the abundant life, really experience it, we can't help but want to share that life with others. Not simply so that they can go to heaven when they die, but just as importantly because they are missing out on so much now. We naturally become witnesses to the truth of Jesus' teachings. Witnesses are simply people who tell others what they have seen and know to be true. Jesus said, "I assure you, those who listen to my message and believe in God who sent me have eternal life" (John 5:24 [NLT]) and "The kingdom of God is among you" (Luke 17:21 [NLT]). When we experience that truth for ourselves we naturally want to share it with others.

The problem is that we create psychological time which then creates psychological fear in our minds and that prevents us from telling others about the eternal, abundant kind of life that is available right now. We create an imaginary future where people reject us for what we have to say or dismiss us as lunatics for believing it. Or, perhaps we're so excited that we try to tell someone who isn't ready to accept it and they do reject us or dismiss us. Then we let that experience, which is now past and over with, create fear in our minds that it will happen again and we allow this event from the dead past to prevent us from acting now.

Jesus knew this could happen and we warned us to be careful about whom we share the truth with. "Don't give what is holy to unholy people. Don't give pearls to swine! They will trample the pearls, then turn and attack you" (Matthew 7:6 [NLT]). This does not mean we are to judge whether others are holy or not. Jesus also warns against doing that! Rather, this means we are to practice the presence of God, wait expectantly for the possibilities God offers us in each moment. As we live the eternal kind of life, others will notice that we have become more peaceful, loving, happy, kind, generous, patient, etc., even when those around us are upset and in turmoil. They will want to know how to live that way, too.

It's similar to someone hearing an accomplished pianist and then asking to take lessons from him or her. The pianist can then show the student what s/he has learned about playing the piano. In the same way, when people see the fruits of the spirit in us, we will be able to teach them what we have learned from Jesus about how to enjoy the conscious awareness of God's presence in the present moment and live effectively in the power of the Holy Spirit.

If we feel we have nothing to offer another person, if we don't know how to help them experience the presence of God right here and right now, we may need to ask ourselves if our faith is simply a collection of intellectual ideas about Jesus and God, or if we are indeed applying what Jesus teaches about having eternal life now.

It may be that we need to step back and regain our focus on the teachings of Jesus. You don' have to take my word for it, probably you should not simply take my word for it, but read what Jesus has to say for yourself and then do what he says to do – no matter how far-fetched it may sound to our twenty-first century minds. If we have confidence in Jesus, if we believe in Jesus, then the least we can do is give it a fair trial. Then we will know whether or not we have something to witness about – something we have experienced and know to be true. Jesus' own brother, James, advises us to do just this. "And remember, it is a message to obey, not just to listen to. If you don't obey, you are only fooling yourself. For if you just listen and don't obey, it is like looking at your face in a mirror but doing nothing to improve your appearance. You see yourself, walk away, and forget what you look like. But if you keep looking steadily into God's perfect law—the law that sets you free—and if you do what it says and don't forget what you heard, then God will bless you for doing it" (James 1:22-25 [NLT]).

Once we experience, really experience the abundant life for ourselves it becomes the most natural thing in the world to tell others about it because we are offering them the truth that sets us free. In that freedom is the salvation of the world. Then we understand and embrace Jesus' words, "Go out and train everyone you meet, far and near, in this way of life, marking them by baptism in the threefold name: Father, Son, and Holy Spirit" (Matthew 28:19 [TMSG]).

Chapter Twelve
Live Life Abundantly!

Jesus tells us, "My purpose is to give life in all its fullness" (John 10:10 [NLT]). Life is meant to be lived. It is a gift from God to be enjoyed, not simply endured. "I said these things to you that my joy may be in you and your joy may be complete" (John 15:11 [NRSV]). Abundant life begins **now**. Too many people are simply marking time, waiting until they get to heaven to start living. As author Susan Ertz says, "Millions long for immortality who do not know what to do with themselves on a rainy Sunday afternoon."

But, if we don't know how to live here in this life, we won't be prepared for life in eternity. If we are bored, miserable, frustrated and unsatisfied here, we will be bored, miserable, frustrated and unsatisfied there. If nothing changes, nothing changes. This is wonderfully illustrated by C.S. Lewis in his book, The Great Divorce. Lewis describes a "grey town" where people who are not ready to enter heaven live after they have died to life on earth. Each day a bus arrives and offers to take them to the top of a nearby cliff where persons they knew during their lifetimes who have gone to heaven visit with them and try to persuade them to return with them to heaven.

Some people in the book are now ready to leave behind the frustrations, misery and disappointments they continue to relive in their minds (the dead past) and allow themselves to be transformed into new creatures as they enter heaven with their friends. But, alas, many refuse to let go of the dead past and the judgments they have made about the past and themselves. They refuse to give up what they think they know and enter the abundant life God has prepared for us "before the foundation of the world" (Ephesians 1:4 [NRSV]).

Emmet Fox used to say, "You are going to live forever – somewhere." Forever is a very long time. It really makes sense to learn how to live joyously and effectively beginning right now, because in reality there is only eternal life. "Very truly, I tell you, whoever believes has eternal life" (John 6:47 [NRSV]).

All we have to do to begin living the eternal kind of life now is to believe Jesus and apply what he taught us. To do that, we have to give up everything we think we know and begin living in the present moment, the eternal now. Now is the only time we ever have to do anything. Real life only happens now. Everything else is an illusion created by our minds. As John Lennon said, "Life is what happens while we're making other plans."

To enter the eternal kind of life, all we have to do is quiet the restless churning of our internal thoughts. Most of us experience about 60,000 thoughts a day, all about either the dead past or an imagined future. The key is to watch for the space between the thoughts and see if we can pay attention to that – because that is where real life happens. That is where we meet God. "For God alone my soul waits in silence" (Psalm 62:1 [NRSV]).

Mother Teresa said, "I always begin my prayer in silence, for it is in the silence of the heart that God speaks. God is the friend of silence – we need to listen to God because it's not what we say but what He says to us and through us that matters."

"Now there was a great wind, so strong that it was splitting mountains and breaking rocks in pieces before the LORD, but the LORD was not in the wind; and after the wind an earthquake, but the LORD was not in the earthquake; and after the earthquake a fire, but the LORD was not in the fire; and after the fire a sound of sheer silence. When Elijah heard it, he wrapped his face in his mantle and went out and stood at the entrance of the cave. Then there came a voice to him" (1 Kings 19:11-13 [NRSV]). In the silence is where we can love God with all our heart, all our soul, all our mind and all our strength. That is where we can love our neighbors as ourselves.

If all this sounds too simple, it might be helpful to recall the story of Naaman, the Syrian (2 Kings 5). Naaman was the very successful and powerful commander of the king's army, but he suffered from leprosy. His wife's maid suggested that he go to the prophet Elisha and ask for healing. Elisha told him to wash himself seven times in the Jordan River and he would be healed. "But Naaman became angry and stalked away . . . 'I expected him to wave his hand over the leprosy and call on the name of the LORD his God and heal me!' . . . So Naaman turned and went away in a rage" (2 Kings 5:11-12 [NLT]).

Naaman was indignant because he was sure that he knew what it would take for Elisha to heal him. How could Elisha insult his intelligence this way? Fortunately for him, his officers challenged him on his preconceived idea, "Sir, if the prophet had told you to do some great thing, wouldn't you have done it? So you should certainly obey him when he says simply to go and wash and be cured!" So Naaman went down to the Jordan River and dipped himself seven times, as the man of God had instructed him. And his flesh became as healthy as a young child's, and he was healed!" (2 Kings 5:13-14 [NLT]).

It really is as simple as living in the space between our thoughts because that is where all real life happens. It's simple, but of course, it isn't easy. "The way to life – to God! – is vigorous and requires total attention" (Matthew 7:14 [TMSG]). It's not easy, but Jesus knew it is possible. The disciples learned how to do it. Paul learned how to do it. We can learn how to do it too.

When we read the New Testament accounts of the early believers with an open mind, the life they lived in the wake of their experience with Jesus is truly remarkable. "A deep sense of awe came over them all, and the apostles performed many miraculous signs and wonders" (Acts 2:43 [NLT]).

If we believe that what Jesus taught is really true, this should not be surprising. "The truth is, anyone who believes in me will do the same works I have done, and even greater works, because I am going to be with the Father. You can ask for anything in my name, and I will do it, because the work of the Son brings glory to the Father. Yes, ask anything in my name, and I will do it!" (John 14:12-14 [NLT])

"Yes, I am the vine; you are the branches. Those who remain in me, and I in them, will produce much fruit. For apart from me you can do nothing. Anyone who parts from me is thrown away like a useless branch and withers. Such branches are gathered into a pile to be burned. But if you stay joined to me and my words remain in you, you may ask any request you like, and it will be granted! My true disciples produce much fruit. This brings great glory to my Father" (John 15:5-8 [NLT]).

"Yes, the way to identify a tree or a person is by the kind of fruit that is produced" (Matthew 7:20 [NLT]).

If we are not living the kind of life characterized by the fruits of the spirit, "love, joy, peace, patience, kindness, generosity, faithfulness, gentleness, and self-control" (Galatians 5:22 [NRSV]) – the eternal kind of life Jesus offers us, it's because we're "not taking God seriously," said Jesus. "The simple truth is that if you had a mere kernel of faith, a poppy seed, say, you would tell this mountain, 'Move!' and it would move. There is nothing you wouldn't be able to tackle" (Matthew 17:20 [TMSG]).

Have confidence in Jesus and believe that he knew what he was talking about and you will find the eternal kind of life – here and now. "You are truly my disciples if you keep obeying my teachings. And you will know the truth, and the truth will set you free" (John 8:31-32 [NLT]).

Let the truth set you free. Believe Jesus.

About the Author

Mark W. Lansberry is an ordained minister in The United Methodist Church currently serving as pastor for Trinity United Methodist Church, in Las Vegas, Nevada (www.tumclv.org). He graduated with a Masters of Divinity degree from the Claremont School of Theology in Claremont, California where he received the Wilshire Preaching Award in 1993. In his preaching and writing (newsletter columns, newspaper articles) he has always strived to use everyday language that the average person on the street can understand. He draws on our shared human and cultural experience through current events, books and movies to illustrate the gospel in ways that allow people to relate to it.

www.ingramcontent.com/pod-product-compliance
Lightning Source LLC
Chambersburg PA
CBHW032022040426
42448CB00006B/701